INSTANT DECOR

Decorating Made Easy

INSTANT DECO

Judy Sheridan, ASID

Park Lane Press
New York • Avenel, New Jersey

OTHER BOOKS BY
JUDY SHERIDAN

Winning Windows

Accessorizing Style

Perfect Picture Hanging

This 1996 edition is published by Park Lane Press, distributed by
Random House Value Publishing, Inc.,
40 Engelhard Avenue, Avenel, New Jersey 07001.

Random House
New York • Toronto • London • Sydney • Auckland
Printed and bound in Singapore

Library of Congress Cataloging-in-Publication Data

Sheridan, Judy.
Instant decor / Judy Sheridan.
p.   cm.
ISBN 0-517-20062-7
1. Interior decoration—Handbooks, manuals, etc. I. Title.
NK2115.S477   1994
747—dc20   94-11870
CIP

8 7 6 5 4 3 2 1

Credits:
Photography by David Regen
Design by Karine Bielefeld
Endpapers: Stroheim & Romann, Inc.

TABLE OF CONTENTS

—◆◇◆—

TRIMS

*W*hen we talk about trims, we're talking about a variety of exciting decorative elements that are available to embellish and beautify your home. Trims include all of the elements found in the details of a well-styled interior, from the narrowest cord used in the seam of a sofa to the wood moulding used to frame a window. In my opinion, no other subject deserves closer attention than the selection of details that go into your interior space.

To use a trim to its full advantage, one must first "see" where using a trim would enhance the object, the surface or the space in general. **Now is the moment to stop and literally take a look around you.** This is our first exercise in developing your ability to "see."

* *Look up at the ceiling. Is there a decorative element between the wall and the ceiling? Or does the wall just meet the ceiling? Would a real crown moulding or a wallpaper border do wonders here? Would a chunky decorative cord?*

* *Look down at the floor. There is probably a base moulding on the wall at the floor line. What condition is it in? Is it plain with little or no detailing? How would you describe it if I asked you to tell me what it looks like? Couldn't it be improved?*

* *Take a look at your upholstered furniture. Look at the seams. Look at the edges where fabric meets a wood frame. Look at the bottom edge of the skirt, if there is one. Aren't these all perfect locations for trim?*

* *Look at the pillows on your furniture, not the seat or back cushions — but the pillows. If there aren't any, you already have a **big hint**. If you have pillows, are they trimmed? Does the trim make you*

Finishing touches on the shawl include tiny silken tassels on each corner and a chunky, tasseled flat braid trim outlining the edges. Also of note is the old Korean wood box, for storing a wig.

feel good when you look at it? If not, isn't it time for a change?

❈ *Lampshades also come under scrutiny in this first step in developing your "eye". Is there anything that could be called trim on the top rim of the shade? What about the bottom rim? If there's trim on the shade, step back and look at the complete lamp. Does it please you? If your answer isn't a strong "yes", then the message is clear: Something needs to be added or changed.*

❈ *Don't overlook walls, especially wall areas in hallways or entries. Aren't these great areas to use mouldings (whether wood or wallpaper), to create panels, dado effects, chair rails or to add to existing mouldings?*

Now you are ready to begin thinking about what types of trims are suitable to use, where to use them, and on which elements. In this chapter we will explore three main classifications of trim and ideas on how to use trim effectively.

A wallpaper border outlining the tile areas in a Bathroom.

The same wallpaper border used with great effect on the ceiling in the Bathroom.

Three main classifications of trims are:

I. Wallpaper borders

II. Trimmings

III. Architectural mouldings

—Tip—

In "designspeak," if it's worth doing, do it with conviction. Otherwise, don't do it at all.

❦ WALLPAPER BORDERS ❧

You can make a real — and often dramatic — change when you use a wallpaper border effectively. I use the word "effectively," because I think most people are too cautious and too conservative when they choose a border. We're going for a little **"oomph"**, here. If you're going to go to the trouble of making a change in your room, let it be a real change. Don't be afraid that it might look funny or wrong. Don't put up a teensy little border, thinking that if it doesn't look good, no one will notice. They will. Even if they don't say it out loud.

General Guidelines

Step 1: To create or emphasize a period or style in the room, use a wallpaper border design that echoes the style of the room.

Step 2: Traditionally, a window or door opening is framed (trimmed) with moulding, either wood or metal. But you can create a new effect or decorate an existing frame with a wallpaper or wood trim. Try the following suggestion when there are no plans for a window treatment, yet where some decoration is desired.

Enhance your existing moulding by simply applying a wallpaper border or a small wood moulding to the wall alongside the moulding that is already there. Follow the line of the existing moulding and create an outline effect with the new trim. If you want to have a decorated feeling without curtains at the window, this is a fabulous way to achieve it.

If the trim around the window or door is substantial or significant, this technique will increase its presence in the room. If this is your goal, you will want to very carefully select a trim that will enhance, not detract, from your existing moulding. Approach your choice with these three guiding precepts:

    a. Stay in the same style.

    b. Don't fight what is there.

    c. Remember, you're **adding to** something that already looks pretty special.

If there is no moulding around the door or window opening, create a moulding. You can do this by using one or two rows of a wallpaper border for the "frame" around a door or window. You might also decide to "really do it right" and add an appropriate *wood trim* to frame the opening. In my opinion, that would be the most satisfying of all.

Step 3: The following suggestions are for those areas where the addition of a border will create a charming, finished look to

your space: (Starred items are illustrated in the accompanying photographs.)

- ❧ *establish a crown moulding at the ceiling **
- ❧ *accent the base moulding in a room **
- ❧ *outline a staircase*
- ❧ *form "panels" in a room*
- ❧ *make a chair rail moulding*
- ❧ *create a dado*
- ❧ *follow the line of tile in a bathroom **
- ❧ *create a backsplash above a countertop*
- ❧ *make a "frame" in which to hang artwork*
- ❧ *finish a cornice board or valance **
- ❧ *create a frame for a bookcase **
- ❧ *trim a screen*
- ❧ *use as a border on a ceiling **

Special Note: For different effects, combine two borders of unequal dimensions and use them together as one border. You can also use a double row of one border, keeping a little space between rows, for a more substantial look. This is especially effective if you have selected a narrow border. See the photograph on page 21.

A dynamic decorative touch in a Bedroom is a 6 inch (15cm) wide wallpaper border applied at the ceiling line and continuing across the cornice board in front of the drapery treatment.

A coordinating narrow wallpaper border used in the same room highlights the base moulding.

Black paint on the interior of a bookcase and an elegant black and gold wallpaper border for the "moulding" combine to produce a striking effect.

—*Tip*—

A trim is always an improvement.

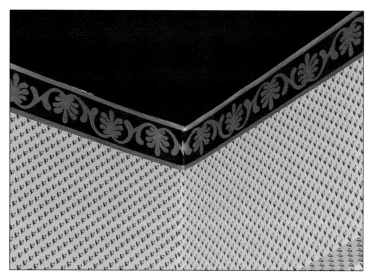

The same black and gold border is repeated at the ceiling, making the most of a small hallway.

❧ TRIMMINGS ☙

Trimmings, with their diversity of style and color, deservedly receive a lot of attention. As we look at our homes with the intent of creating an inviting interior, decorative trims are an easy and elegant way to give rooms a professional finish.

Trims can be both decorative and practical. You may be interested to know that the origin of using fringe on the edges of draperies is based on a very practical need. Fabrics were extremely expensive centuries ago and to protect the edges of these precious fibers from the harmful rays of the sun coming through the window, someone designed a "trimming".

The invention of gimps and braids came about as a way to hide the tacks (and later, staples) that were used to attach fabric to furniture frames and walls. Cord inserted

in the seams of upholstered furniture — especially to the edges of seat cushions and decorative pillows — protected the fabric edges from soilage and wear. Even though trimmings were initially used to answer practical concerns, it is no accident that they have always been enjoyed as ornamentation. I love knowing that, centuries later, they still serve the same purposes. Practical and ornamental. Decidedly the best of both worlds.

What a difference the addition of a small trim can make! A cottony gimp trim with scalloped edge is glued to the top and bottom rims of a standard black paper lampshade.

In the chart below, look at the suggestions for using trims based on the category of uses for which they are best suited. Then look at the photographs in this chapter to aid you in developing an ability for placing trims in inviting and innovative spots.

Care Tip: Fringe, especially fringe with tassels, must be steamed before you start to work with it. Steam it with your steam iron by holding the iron just above the fringe — it is very important that the hot soleplate of your iron does not touch the fringe itself — letting the steam penetrate into the fibers. This process plumps up the fibers in the fringe so that they look full and neat with no stray or wrinkled strands. Use a sharp pointed pair of scissors to clip off any unsightly strands or extraneous fibers.

Style	Description	Uses
Gimp	Flat, narrow woven textile; ³⁄₈"(1cm) – ¹⁄₂"(1.5cm) in width; also made with a cord sewn in the center or on the edge.	To cover upholstery tacks, staples in wood frame furniture; to hide staples and finish upholstered walls and screens; to trim lampshades, pillows.
Braid	Flat, ribbon-like woven textile; ⁵⁄₈"(2cm) – 4"(10cm) in width; made in various patterns; the edges can be cut, looped, scalloped, or straight.	To apply to the edges of draperies, table skirts, decorative screens, pillows, cornices, valances and the skirts on upholstered furniture.
Cord	Yarns that are twisted together; ³⁄₁₆"(0.5cm) – 1"(3cm) in width; called rope when larger than 1" (3cm).	To insert in the seams of upholstered furniture, cushions, draperies, tableskirts and pillows; must have a flange or tape sewn to the edge of the cord to be inserted into seam; to use without a tape or flange instead of gimp or braid on wall upholstery, or furniture, or along top edge of valances or cornices.
Fringe	Cut, loop, tassel or bullion; sizes range from 1" (3cm) to 12" (30cm) long.	To be used more decoratively by applying to draperies, swags and jabots, valances, cornices, upholstered furniture, pillows, tableskirts, cushions, lampshades or the edges of skirts on upholstered furniture; by inserting in the seams of pillows, cushions, draperies, swags and jabots, or table skirts.

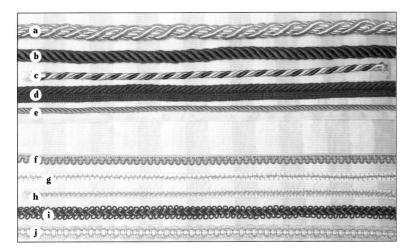

Top photo:
a, b, c: Assorted cords
d, e: Cords with tape
f, g, h, i, j: Gimp trims

Middle photo:
a: Bell-shape tassel fringe
b, c: Loop fringe
d, e: Cut fringe
f: Scallop loop fringe
g: Tassel fringe
h: Flat braid
i, j: Scallop loop fringe on
flat braid

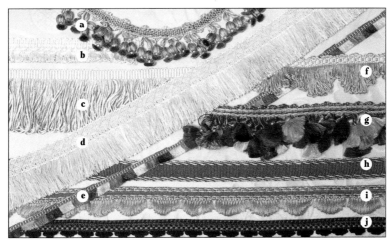

Bottom photo:
a, b, c: Bullion fringe,
assorted sizes
d: Bullion fringe with
added cord swag,
tassel "hangers"

*A favorite method of mine: the layering of two trims, one on top of the other.
Trimming the bottom edge of a valance, a flat braid with scalloped edges is sewn
together with a short bullion fringe and applied as one trim.*

Another way to steam trims — and this technique is also very handy for freshening trims that have been in your home for a few years — is to fill a kettle with water, bring it to a boil, and pass the trims over the steam emitting from the spout.

Use a clothes brush and a toothbrush to neaten fringe on items too big to bring to the kettle and where using a steam iron is unwieldy. Just comb it as you would animal fur. Once a client saw me doing this and thought I had left the planet. But I love brushing trims; there is something deeply satisfying about it. Besides, the trims look so much better afterwards. With small trimmed items or single tassels, you can brush or comb them while holding the article over the steaming kettle and obtain excellent results.

Special Tip: One technique I like is to use two different fringes layered together and applied as one trim. You will be surprised at the singular effect achieved when you do this. And don't be put off by the cost. Frequently, the total cost of the two trims together is less than the price of a single, heavier fringe. Using one trim alone never has the impact of using two.

Without overdoing it, you can, of course, use more than two trims. Much depends on where the trims are being used, but you can decide how many look good together. This technique will give you a much more sumptuous look, and is especially effective on lampshades and pillows, as well as draperies and table skirts.

I think the final word here is sumptuous. Trimmings always add a sumptuous, elegant air to the objects on which they are applied. They can add a richness that ranges from subtle understatement to bold flamboyance, but it is a quality absolutely required for a successfully interpreted room.

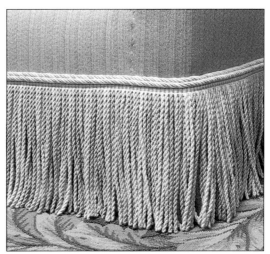

Above: Another way to layer trims — use two rows of the same long bullion fringe on an upholstered piece for a superbly languorous look.

Left: A simple gimp trim gives a standard paper shade a custom-finished appearance.

ARCHITECTURAL
MOULDINGS

Crown Mouldings

For those of you unfamiliar with the term, this is moulding that is installed at the highest point or uppermost part of a room, at or near the ceiling. Simple or ornate, narrow or wide, moulding installed at the ceiling line of a room is referred to as crown moulding.

—Tip—

The addition of ANY moulding at the ceiling line will improve the appearance of a room.

You might not be adept at working with this type of moulding installation, since it involves a certain degree of woodworking expertise. If that's the case, it's best to think of having crown mouldings professionally installed.

However, if you can cut a clean mitered corner, know the difference between an inside and outside corner, can butt two pieces of moulding together into a clean join, can neatly fill corners of moulding, and you have a ready supply of patience, then I encourage you to put up crown moulding yourself, using a single-piece moulding.

*A classic, and ever beautiful,
egg and dart crown moulding.*

*To effectively simulate a crown
moulding, use two rows of the
same wallpaper border, with a
little spacing between the rows,
at the ceiling.*

Budget considerations, of course, are also something to consider. If price is a problem, and if there are other valid reasons for not using a real moulding, I have another suggestion. If you have your heart set on using a moulding at the ceiling because you know it will create the effect you want, use a wallpaper border instead. Try a combination of two different borders (of different widths, but harmonizing styles) to produce a strong statement; or double up on a single border, which means using two rows of it together, applied as a single border. (See photo on page 21.)

You might also want to try using a **small** wood moulding in combination with a paper border as illustrated in the photograph on page 24. This suggestion is certainly more affordable than the full crown moulding treatment, and much easier to handle.

If, after considering the options I've discussed, you decide to use a real moulding, there is a great selection available in composition (or polymer) patterns. You will find that it is cost-effective to use these composition mouldings. They are lightweight and ready for paint or stain.

For a truly customized moulding, try the "layering technique" by incorporating two or more different wood mouldings. Keep in mind that this type of moulding will need filler pieces added to it, to hold it all together and will require a drawing. But the result is very special and worth every bit of the investment, which in this case is not just financial. If you need proof of how terrific a combination moulding looks, refer to the drawing and photograph on the next page.

There are several ways to finish a crown moulding: wood stain or paint, or a combination of the two. If you like the idea of a wood stain, and the moulding you select is a composition product, make sure the stain is a non-penetrating wood stain and follow the particular manufacturer's instructions on the types of finishes recommended for the product. A very elegant way to paint a crown moulding is in a faux bois (fake wood) or faux marbre (fake marble) finish. Depending on how good the qualifications are of the person executing the faux painting, it can be hard to tell that the moulding is painted, especially looking at it from eye level in the room.

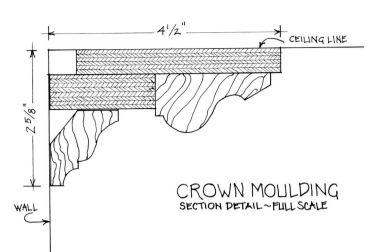

4½"

CEILING LINE

2⅝"

WALL

CROWN MOULDING
SECTION DETAIL ~ FULL SCALE

Diagram 1.
The drawing of a crown mould-
ing, in cross section, showing the
layers of two stock mouldings
with required filler pieces.

Right: The finished crown
moulding, shown in Diagram 1.,
as it looks painted and installed.

Diagram 2:
The colors of the "stripes" on the
moulding were worked out on
paper first, and tried on a sam-
ple piece of moulding, before the
finish coats of paint were
applied.

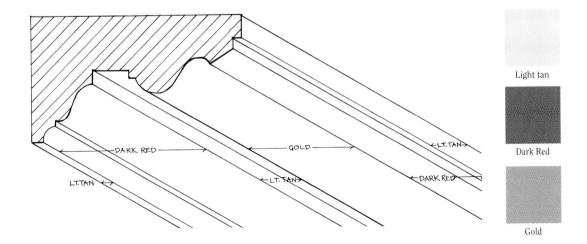

DARK RED

GOLD

LT. TAN

LT. TAN

LT. TAN

DARK RED

LT. TAN

Light tan

Dark Red

Gold

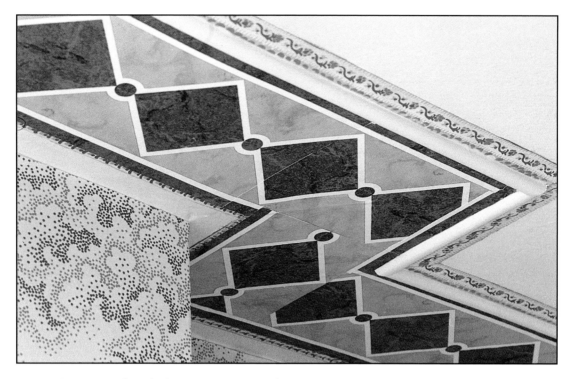

Inventiveness is often the key to interesting solutions. Here, to update a previously installed border on a ceiling, a new border was pasted on top of the original. A small half-round moulding was then added to camouflage the gap between the different widths of the two wallpaper borders.

I love the way a large crown moulding looks when it is painted. It is very nice to be able to use colors taken from the color scheme of the room and emphasize them by taking them up into the moulding. A crown moulding can look spectacular painted in a single color (one that is different from the wall and ceiling colors.) Equally spectacular is using two colors or, depending on the size of the moulding itself and your room decor, as many as four colors. It is my experience that three colors work very well. The crown moulding on the preceding page used a total of four colors very effectively.

Painting moulding in this fashion is literally painting stripes on it. If you are accustomed to doing your own painting, you will find painting crown mouldings to be a very creative and satisfying endeavor. On the other hand, you may decide to hire someone else to do the painting. At least you now know how to approach this kind of project and can make an informed decision.

The bottom line here is how you want your space to look. I always advise a client to come up with a price. What is it really worth to you? If something you really want is going to cost $1,650.00 — which would translate into a $1.50 per day for the next three years — and it would give you much pleasure every time you looked at it, wouldn't you say "yes" and pay the $1.50 per day? Consider it. Try thinking in terms of the pleasure it will add to your life.

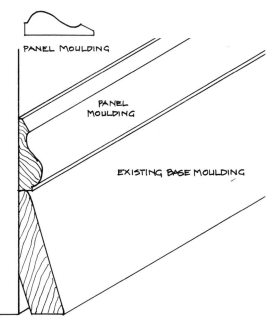

PANEL MOULDING

PANEL MOULDING

EXISTING BASE MOULDING

Diagram 3. A cross section of panel moulding, above; and below, the way in which the panel moulding was used: installed above an existing base moulding of clam shell trim.

Base Mouldings

Here's one of the blanket statements that I make from time to time, based on my experience in the interior design business:

If your residence is at least 20 years old or has a build-up of at least a half dozen layers of paint, the best thing you can do to improve the general appearance of your space is to rip out the existing base moulding and replace it with new moulding.

I can hear the howls. I know that means a lot of work, and it is not inexpensive either, but NOTHING will give your room a more crisp, architectural quality or supply a more professional finish, than new base moulding.

— *Tip* —

Always keep in mind: It's the details that make the difference.

Here are some of the reasons why:

❀ *New base moulding creates a clean finish line where the moulding meets the wall.*

❀ *It also creates a clean finish line where the base moulding meets the floor.*

❀ *Old wires, paint nicks, dents, and lumps are eliminated.*

❀ *TV cable, telephone and speaker wires can all be concealed behind the new base.*

❀ *A new base makes the walls look as if they were newly built.*

❀ *You can choose a moulding designed to suit the style of your decor.*

❀ *A strong style of moulding adds immeasurably to the professional, finished quality of your room.*

Changing an Existing Moulding:

Let's talk about ways in which to improve your existing base moulding without going to the expense of replacing what you have:

1. Add a small wood moulding to your existing base. This increases the height of the base moulding and adds to its importance in the room.

2. Install the new piece of moulding on top of the moulding you already have in place; prepare it for painting, and paint it in the same color as your existing base. Or paint it in a contrast color.

3. Another effective way to change your existing base moulding (if you don't want to use a wood moulding) is to use a wallpaper border in the same way as you would a second piece of wood moulding. Place it just above the existing moulding. Then paint the moulding either in a contrasting color to the wallpaper border or in a color that harmonizes with it. See a photo of this technique on the bottom of page 13.

Door Panel Mouldings

Adding applied mouldings to doors is an easy, yet often overlooked, method of bringing about a **significant** change in a room. I often have a hard time convincing someone to "**see**" the change that this particular detail will make in the feeling and quality of a room. But that is what we designers do best. **We see.**

1. All doors can be improved by the addition of mouldings, including cabinet, cupboard, and closet doors.

2. Look at the illustrations of generic types of panel mouldings on page 27. Identify the style category that you relate to. Your choices are:

   ❀ *Conservative*

   ❀ *Traditional*

   ❀ *Period Style*

   ❀ *Transitional*

3. If you have doors that are blank, faceless, flat surfaces, then select a style of moulding. Next, either break out the

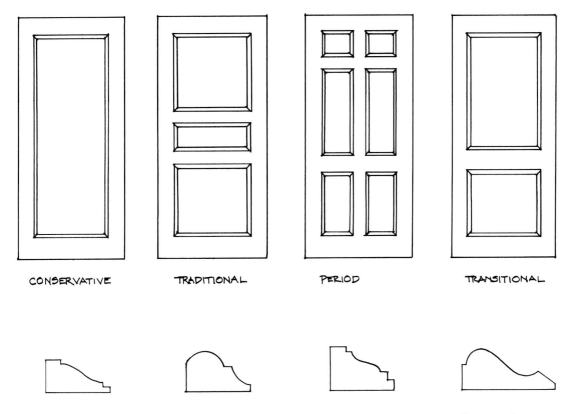

CONSERVATIVE   TRADITIONAL   PERIOD   TRANSITIONAL

Diagram 4. Four applications of panel moulding used to create different panel effects on doors: In each version the moulding is shown in cross section underneath the corresponding door.

tools yourself or find someone to install the mouldings for you.

4. Once the mouldings are installed, the doors need to be refinished in whichever medium you choose: stain, lacquer, or paint.

It is hard to understand the significant impact that something as simple as the addition of mouldings to doors can have, but that is really what decorating is all about.

To take it even further, I would say that all of the seemingly small, simple elements that we have discussed in this chapter serve the same purpose. I have tried to illustrate changes that are not only realistic to undertake, but will result in increased visual pleasure in your decor. The cumulative effect of these changes should create an atmosphere that says "substantial" and "quality." Isn't that what we want in our home environment?

KEY TASSELS, TASSELS, AND CHAIR TIES

I know of no faster, easier way to update your surroundings than to add tassels to your furnishings. Used judiciously, tassels, key tassels, and chair ties provide an instant pick-me-up and stylish air wherever you place them. Think of them as little teasers...they seem to brighten whatever you attach them to. They also brighten your outlook. If you are unsure of the differences between tassels, key tassels and chair ties, refer to the photograph on pages 36 and 37. Also, you will see several examples of ways that we have used these small charmers in the photos on the next few pages. First, study the possibilities and consider spots in your own home where you would like to add tassels, key tassels, and chair ties.

The first place to look for tassels, key tassels, and chair ties is in a home furnishings or fabric store. If you don't know of one, look in the Yellow Pages for a listing. You might also try contacting a decorator, decorating shop or an upholstery shop that has a decorating service. Through any of these sources, you should be able to select and/or order these items.

Tassels, key tassels, and chair ties are available in a large array of colors, woven in silk, cotton, rayon, wool or combinations of these fibers. Select a color that will complement your overall color scheme: this can be a soft, harmonizing color or a color totally opposite from what you already have in the room. Don't be afraid to choose a color that will add a little punch or sparkle. Remember: you're adding an accent and the color you choose should be just that — an accent.

❧ KEY TASSELS ☙

Key tassels are one of the easiest items to add to existing decor, because you don't need to do anything in the way of preparation. You simply use them "as is." Just take the string on the tassel and place it on or through a cabinet pull or drawer handle, open up the loop, pass the tassel through the loop, and gently pull the tassel until the string tightens around the piece of hardware. Likely locations for a key tassel are on the drawer of a desk, table, dresser, or chest. Now, if your piece of furniture has a key, attach the key tassel to it. Remember, a single tassel on a piece of furniture is always best, unless it's something like an armoire or cabinet which has two doors. In that case, you will want to put a tassel on each handle.

Here's a suggestion for that piece of furniture that has a keyhole but no key. This applies to any item with a keyhole: boxes, trunks, clock cases, or drawers being likely examples. First, locate a hardware store that sells decorative hardware. Frequently their stock will include ornamental keys. If they have decorative brass or steel keys, look through the assortment of keys

to find a style that will be appropriate for your piece of furniture, and then determine if there is a key that will fit into your existing lock opening.

Of course, it makes sense to attempt to remove the lock from the piece of furniture in order to have it with you. But that may not be practical, either for you or for the item. If the lock case slips out easily after you have removed the hardware that holds it in place, then, by all means, take it with you. But if it doesn't come out easily, don't risk damaging the lock or your furniture. Simply face the fact that you will have to bring the key(s) back to the piece of furniture and try it (them).

Another possibility to consider is to search for authentic old keys in used furniture stores and antique shops. Quite often, store owners wind up with an assortment of odd keys, most of which are never of any use for operating a lock. However, these keys will often fit an old lock, and will be most acceptable for that added decorative touch.

All you want this key to do is fit in the keyhole opening securely enough to attach a key tassel to it. You can fudge a bit if it's not quite the right size. Far more important

Looped around the center handle on a chest of drawers, this plump little key tassel adds a playful note to the decor.

Facing Page: A wondrous array of old and new keys and attached key tassels.

is the way the key looks. Does the style suit your piece of furniture? If it doesn't, plan to continue your search until you find just the right style of key. This may seem to you a rather unimportant issue, but attention to detail is the principle idea behind the whole concept of design. Adopting this approach will make the difference between an interior that is just "okay," and one that really has a certain style. **Attention to detail.** I will say it over and over.

If you're happy with the style of the key, but it's a little wobbly in the lock, try putting a tiny bit of "silly putty" or florist's clay into the opening to secure the key. If that doesn't work, you may decide that you should really have a key to operate the lock. If so, take the ornamental key to a locksmith and have him produce a key that will fit and operate the lock. Yes, your locksmith really can do this. He may even appreciate the opportunity to practice his skills, since I doubt he gets this kind of request very often.

Many creative touches delight me, but I'm especially partial to key tassels. Here are some suggestions for places to put them that I think are particularly attractive:

❀ *a doorknob*
❀ *the handle of a medicine chest*

❧ *the bottom piece of a hanging light fixture or wall sconce*

❧ *attached to the pull chain of a light fixture*

Be a little whimsical and try tying one onto the handle of:

❧ *a favorite pitcher*

❧ *a pair of scissors*

❧ *a basket*

❧ *the pull-up cord of a window shade*

❧ *the top of a birdcage*

Let me add one more word on the subject of key tassels before we move on to tassels. Because of their popularity, key tassels are made in a range of sizes. To give you an idea, the smallest ones are about 1½" (38mm) long (the size is the length of the tassel only, not the length of the loop), and go up to 3"(76mm) and 4½"(114mm) long; from short, thin ones to those with fat, puffy bodies. Pick a style and size that is consistent with where the key tassel will hang. A slim, longish one tied onto the key in a tea caddy would be very elegant looking, while a short plump key tassel would convey just the right note on the end of a chain or on a desk drawer handle.

❧ TASSELS ❧

Tassels differ from key tassels in only a few ways. The tassel is attached to a cord, not a loop, so different methods are necessary to attach it. They can be used with or without a rosette. Also, the overall scale of a tassel is larger than that of a key tassel; but today they are made in small and even miniature versions. This enables you to use them in a wide variety of locations. The main difference is in the silhouette: a key tassel looks like a little tutu on the end of a string, while a tassel maintains a straighter, almost equal dimension from top to bottom.

Bear these differences in mind when you decide to use tassels instead of key tassels. To attach tassels, you'll need to get out the glue, pins, or a needle and thread. The particular method you use to attach them depends on the location and how permanent the application is going to be.

Let me suggest some places that could really use a tassel:

❧ *the front panel on the arm of a sofa or chair (Glue, pin, or hand tack.)*

In full glory, a perfect tassel attached to the center of a decorative cornice.

❉ the center at the top of a fabric shade, such as a balloon, Austrian or Roman shade (Hand tack or pin.)

❉ either end of a fabric valance or upholstered cornice, at the top on the outer edge (Glue, pin, or hand tack.)

❉ the center of a fabric valance or upholstered cornice, at or close to the top (Glue, pin, or hand tack.)

❉ all four corners of a pillow (Hand tack.)

❉ in the intersections of a balloon shade, at the bottom (see the illustration for this version) (Hand tack or pin.)

❉ the upper outside corner of a shower curtain (this should look as though you would pull the shower curtain across with the tassel, which, of course, you could if you attach it securely enough) (Hand tack.)

❉ the top of a Christmas tree could use two tied together with a real velvet ribbon for a bow (Tie with wire or string.)

❉ the point where a curtain tie-back attaches to a wall (Hand tack or pin to tie-back, or glue to the wall.)

❉ the outer corners of a bed coverlet, shawl, or table runner (Hand tack.)

Now look around your interior...slowly. Look at your walls, furniture, and windows. Don't you see many places where you could use a tassel?

Next two pages: A collection of key tassels, tassels, tassels with rosettes, and chair ties.
    Key tassels: A, F, G, O
    Tassels: E, I, L, M
    Tassels with rosettes: B, C, J, K, N
    Chair ties: D, H

❦ CHAIR TIES ❧

Aptly named, chair ties, are designed to tie a seat cushion to a chair. Designers have found other delightful ways in which to use them, but we'll talk about those later. For the moment, let's talk about our original need for chair ties. If your chairs already have seat cushions on them, consider updating them by changing the existing chair ties to new ones.

I've met many clients who were relieved to learn what to do with loose, unattached seat cushions and how easy it is to keep them from moving around. Stools with seat cushions can always benefit from this treatment, and will always be more decorative with the addition of ties. You might even decide to get a seat cushion for a stool now that you have a way to keep the seat cushion in place when you sit on it. After attaching the ties to the cushion (and plan on using a tie for each leg), just secure the tie around the leg as you would do for a chair.

To change an existing cushion, carefully cut off whatever type of tie is on the cushion now. Take the new chair

tie, locate the center of the cord; then hand tack the cord at this center point to one of the outer corners of the cushion. Once the cord is attached, tie the cord around the leg of the chair in a knot or a bow. Depending on the style of the chair, and the cushion, plan to use ties on all four legs. Sometimes this physically can't be done, but your chair will let you know.

So far we have been using cords with attached tassels. Usually found in a 27" length, it's not unusual to find them slightly shorter or longer. A longer length will make a nice big bow.

Happily, chair ties can be made from almost any type of ribbon or fabric. If you opt for ribbon, think of adding a small tassel to each end to add extra polish to the finished tie. I find fabric is an easier choice. Making strips of fabric to use as chair ties is relatively simple. Also, it gives you total freedom in your choice of color.

When choosing color, don't try to match a particular color. For example, your existing cushions will already have a fabric, and most likely, a

Chair ties and welting of "contrast" fabric used to accent the green pattern fabrics of the seat cushions on chairs in a Kitchen.

Cord and tassel chair ties give a polished look to a loose seat cushion on a wood frame chair.

welt or cord in the seams that may add yet another hue. Try for a neutral compromise or an absolute contrast.

In another vein, here are some ways to use them that give pretty touches in your home:

❧ *Tie a chair tie into a bow and place it on the upper rim of a lampshade — guaranteed to add instant charm!*

❧ *Try a chair tie wrapped around a napkin for an elegant version of a napkin ring. Use a loose knot or bow and try two of the ties together in different colors for even greater panache.*

❧ *Gather several chair ties knotted into a bow and glue-tack or sew them at spaced intervals along the top edge of a tableskirt, right at the top of the table.*

❧ *Attach a "bow" to the center of the front of each arm on a sofa or loveseat.*

❧ *Spiff up some of your throw pillows — placing one at each corner of the pillow.*

❧ *You can also tie the chair tie to form a single loop. With this version, plan to use them in groups of three to seven. Now you can:*

❧ *Cluster the ties at the end corners of a drapery valance*

or cornice board. Use glue, staples, or thread to do this.

❧ *Add a cluster of them to the center of your valance or cornice.*

❧ *If you have a bed with posts, try tying groups of the ties onto each post up at the top, using the loop version in combination with the bow version and in a mix of colors.*

In these last three suggestions, don't be afraid to go overboard. Using more chair ties, rather than less, will produce far better results — as you will note in the photographs on the right.

When you're using differently colored chair ties together, follow the guidelines below. They'll help direct you in selecting your colors:

Above: Diagram 5a. A chair tie tied with a loop and a knot.

Left: Diagram 5b. A chair tie tied in a bow.

Facing Page: Chair ties, in a soft mix of colors, tied onto the bed posts and clustered at the corners of a balloon shade in a Bedroom. Inset photo shows the chair ties tied in single loops, their colors selected from the colors in the chintz fabric pattern.

a. Do you already have a defined group of colors in the room that are found in a fabric, painting, or rug? Choose from three to five of the most interesting of these colors to use as the color mix for the chair ties.

b. If you don't have anything in the room to go on and you don't know where to begin, consider adding a new element to the room that you relate to strongly. Use that object's colors as your starting point for chair tie selection.

c. If your color scheme runs toward neutral tones, select three or four closely related colors and add a "punch" or accent color. An example of this would be white, cream, and pale pink with a strong green as the accent.

For a zippy effect, always remember that the colors should either complement your surroundings or be in total contrast to them.

One of my favorite ideas for using a chair tie is to tie and loosely knot one around a favorite book, such as an appointment or note book…it makes an ordinary object look a little special. Use one as a bookmark, or tie one into a bow around an envelope and make a "gift" out of a card, note, or money folder. I want you to start thinking of using these ties in places where you are accustomed to using a rubber band, ribbon, or string. If you can start to "see" in this manner, you'll have the right approach. These small, but important, elements will guide you into boldly displaying your own unique style in your surroundings.

Care Tip: All tassels will benefit from a good steaming before you attach them. After a few years, steam older tassels again to refresh them and return them to their original plump state. For more complete information regarding steaming, reread the Care Tip for fringes in Chapter One, pages 16 – 18.

Little touches, including the various tassels we have covered in this chapter, mean much to the person living in a thoughtfully decorated space. The little things that the eye chances to fall upon, the small elements of beauty that nourish one in a quiet moment; these will trigger a memory years later that surprisingly can remind one of an entire room. A tassel can bring an unexpected sensuousness to an otherwise ordinary space.

A chair tie tied in a bow, leaving a loop big enough to go around the top rim of a lampshade.

Royal blue and golden hued chair ties, tied in single loops, are pinned on alternating pleats in the blue toile draperies. More blue chair ties are used to create a swag between each pleat. Then the chair ties, tied in loops and tied together, are attached to the outer corners, ending in soft trailing clusters of both colors.

LAMPSHADES

*T*his chapter will explore various ways to give your rooms a professional touch by simply trimming your lampshades. With this information, you may even consider adding new lampshades to light fixtures that until now, you hadn't realized were without shades. At the very least you'll consider replacing existing shades that have long been neglected. With fresh eyes, you will see how trimming lampshades can affect the overall feeling of a room.

*T*his is where the fun begins. Fun, because all it takes to change the way a lampshade looks, is some trim, scissors, glue, and a little creativity. It's like tying a ribbon on a package. You don't need talent, brain power, or developed skills — just a dollop of patience and your eyes to guide you into making the right choices with your materials and colors.

*T*o make a fast effective change in the way a lamp looks is easier than you think. Take any one of your lampshades — regardless of what the shade is made: fabric, paper, or synthetic material — and add a trim to the top and bottom of the shade. Now isn't that simple? And what a difference it will make. The photos that accompany this chapter will show you how effective those differences can be.

*W*hen I use the word *trim,* I refer to two basic categories:

1. Flat, narrow woven textiles, $^{3}/_{8}$" – $^{1}/_{2}$" (1-1.27cm) wide, which include gimp, flat braid, tape, and ribbon

2. Fringe — which generally speaking, is a woven band with an attached decorative element. The "decorative element" can be a soft brush of fringe, loops, cut

Photographs, before (left), and after (right), show the differences between an untrimmed lampshade, and the same lampshade, trimmed. What makes the difference is the pale yellow cord on the top rim and a green, white and gold cut fringe on the bottom.

loops, tassels, scalloped edging, or any of these in combination.

Special Note: For best results, the band of the trim should be no more than $\frac{1}{2}$" wide. When you're fastening a trim to a shade, you will find that anything wider tends to stand away from the shade, and you won't be able to get it to follow the curve of the shade very well.

When I use the term "contrast trim," I am referring to any trim that is different in texture and/or color from what it is being applied to.

Color: The color of the trim should contrast with the color of the shade, but still be a color that will work with the other colors in the room. You might ask: What possible effect could the color of a tiny little trim have on the overall look of the room? And that's a good question.

While the color of the trim might seem to be an insignificant detail, in the end, it has everything to do with the overall effect of a room. You might find this hard to accept, but I assure you that it really does matter.

*Left: A lamp, purchased in a thrift shop, came with an old 10" (20.5cm) harp and the original decorative finial. **Right:** A new cut-corner square shade, correctly proportioned, sitting on a smaller harp, 6¹/₂" (10.7cm) high. **Facing page:** The addition of a very fine bullion fringe on the bottom edge and a gold and white gimp trim, used on top and bottom, bestows a certain elegance on the lampshade.*

Keep in mind:

* ❈ *The color should contrast with the shade fabric*

* ❈ *Or blend in with the shade*

* ❈ *Better results are usually obtained with a contrast*

If you're looking at trims for the first time, you may be surprised at the sparsity of colors available in any given style. It may strike you, as it often does me, that the color range of a trim is so limited that you can't imagine using any one of them!

> ## —*Tip*—
>
> *Ignore how something is **supposed** to look. Try something different.*

Usually, when I find myself in this situation, I have to choose *something*. And surprisingly, I find that when I force myself to make a decision that I'm not crazy about, and hope that somehow it will look alright in the end, I'm amazed that it does!

Somehow the color always seems to be right on target. So take heart, plunge in and make a selection.

It's time to take a close look at **your** lampshades. Wouldn't trimming any one of them add a finishing touch to your room? And wouldn't this be a good time to think of replacing those shades that aren't in mint condition? Sometimes it is so difficult to be honest when it comes to our own things.

—*Tip*—

Learn to be dispassionate about your own possessions. Act as if they belong to someone else.

If you can honestly apply any of the following adjectives to your lampshade, then my friend, it is time to replace it:

* *bent*
* *dented*
* *torn*
* *faded*
* *scorched*
* *mis-sized*

Here's another question that is related to this subject. Do you have wall sconces or a chandelier with little "candles" that are without shades — where the bare lightbulbs are showing?

I find uncovered lightbulbs to be most bothersome. Whether frosted or clear, these small lightbulbs, called candelabra lights, are hard on the eyes—even when the fixture is on a dimmer.

For some reason many people do not think of finishing a chandelier or wall sconce with lampshades. Perhaps they don't want to go to the extra expense of adding shades or maybe they think that the fixture is okay without shades. In my opinion it isn't. Fortunately, adding small "chandelier" shades to these light fixtures will:

* *greatly improve the appearance of the light fixture,*
* *add a real decorative touch to any room,*

Diagram 6a.(above) A shirred fabric shade, gimp trim on top rim, small tassel fringe on the bottom rim.
Diagram 6b. (left) A plain surface (fabric or paper) shade with a gimp trim used on both top and bottom rims.

❧ *soften the lighting, and at the same time,*

❧ *greatly benefit the visual comfort of the room occupants.*

Isn't that a nice dividend for such a small addition?

Chandelier shades are readily available in white and ivory fabrics, and black and patterned papers. They readily work into a color scheme that will complement most situations. They are easy and fun to work with because they are so diminutive: the most common size in this type of shade is one that is 4"(10cm) high, with a 3"(8cm) diameter top and 4"(10cm) bottom. Larger and smaller variations of this basic size certainly exist.

Here is my approach:

❧ *Do a test run.*

❧ *Bring home two or three different size shades.*

❧ *Try them on the fixture.*

❧ *Decide which is the best size.*

These small shades look especially festive when you use a hanging type trim (such as a tassel fringe) for the bottom, and a narrower tape trim for the top. In other words, you can use different trims, top and bottom.

We'll next review three basic types of trimming techniques, suitable for almost all lampshade styles and sizes. While three types of trimming techniques may seem surprisingly few, with the vast variety of trims and the different styles of lampshades to put them on, you will be delighted when you see how different and exciting the results can be. Guaranteed!

❧ TYPE 1 ❧

Top and bottom, trimmed.

This is the easiest category of lampshade trimming and applies to all lampshades. You can start by determining how much trim you will need for the shade. If you have decided to use the same trim, top and bottom, here is how to proceed:

ESTIMATING
the Amount of Trimming

1. Measure the *diameter* of the shade at the top and at the bottom.

2. Add the two figures together.

3. Multiply that figure by 3.14*. This gives you the circumference of the shade rim. *(pi=the ratio, 3.141592+; pi, when multiplied by the diameter of a circle, gives you the circumference of the circle).

4. Add at least one inch (3cm) for each rim to your total measurement to allow for overlapping the ends and ease in working. Add more if your comfort level calls for a larger margin of error.

5. If you're working in inches, take the total figure and divide this number by 36, to determine the yards needed. Round this number up to the nearest $1/4$-yard, since trims and fabrics are sold in $1/4$-yard increments. Example: a figure of 44" would be rounded up to 45", which equals $1\,1/4$ yards.

6. If you are using the metric system, once you have added the circumference of the rim, together with the extra allowance, round this figure to the next centimeter for the total amount of trimming you need to purchase.

(Note: A metric conversion chart is located at the back of the book, page 94.)

Special Note: An unusually pretty trimming technique for a lampshade (paper or fabric) is to use a ribbon (taffeta, grosgrain, silk, etc., $1/2$" to $3/4$"[1–2cm] wide), preferably one that has a pattern, stripe, or plaid, and shirr or pleat it in the sewing machine. Your line of stitching can run

A lovely 5-arm chandelier with lampshades created from the remaining pieces of fabric and ribbon trim used in the window treatment of a Bedroom.

How pretty the pattern of this sheer fabric looks with the light from the chandelier glowing softly inside the shade.

A close-up of the fabric, which is glued along the top and bottom edges of a basic beige paper shade; the ribbon is also glued to the shade and hides the cut edges of the fabric.

either along the center of the ribbon or at the edge. Glue or hand sew the shirred or pleated ribbon to the top and bottom rims of your lampshade.

Different trims, top and bottom.

In my opinion, a more decorative effect can be achieved by using two different trims: choosing a narrow gimp trim for the top rim and, for the bottom, a trim with an edging to it — something that hangs down a bit, such as small tassels or a brush edge.

Keep in mind that in order to maximize the effect, the two trims should either match in color, or one color needs to pre-dominate — both top and bottom — if several colors are involved.

The procedure for measuring remains the same as Steps 1–6 on pages 51 – 52, except you should measure and calculate the top rim and bottom rim separately.

1. It is essential to wash your hands first.

2. Set up your work space to allow yourself plenty of elbow room.

3. Keep a damp sponge and several paper towels at your side to take care of glue drips and fingers that become sticky.

4. Keep the shade on the lamp. But set the finial aside, because you want to be able to turn the shade easily on the center screw as you work around it.

5. For smaller, chandelier type shades — ones having a clip-on feature — you will probably find that it's easier to work with the shade in one hand.

6. Line up the trim that you are applying with a band or edge on the shade rim, so that you have a guide to follow. This enables you to keep a very even line as you attach the new trim.

7. Once you have your trim(s), get out the white glue bottle or your hot glue gun and simply dot the glue onto the shade along the edge, spacing the dots of glue approximately $\frac{1}{2}$" to 1" apart (1–3cm). Don't get too far ahead of yourself with the glue before starting to apply the trim. The weight of the trim and time it takes for the glue to adhere will determine the spacing.

8. The tricky part, you will find, is to maintain an even beading of glue, and not use too much of it, as it will tend to drop off the edge of the shade onto your work surface — or worse, onto the shade itself.

9. As you position the trim on the edge of the shade, hold it so that the glue has a chance to adhere before you proceed.

10. Place the cut edge of the trim even with a seam on the shade, or at whichever point you consider the back of the shade to be. As you come around to where you started, plan to overlap the ends of the trim about $\frac{1}{2}$" (1 cm) or less.

Special Note: If you are using very sharp scissors or an X-Acto knife, make a very clean cut on both ends of the trim so that they butt up to each other, instead of overlapping. It's a much cleaner, more professional look. Now, very carefully dab a bit of glue onto the cut end of the trim so that it doesn't unravel; this will also ensure that it stays in place.

⟪ TYPE 2 ⟫

Vertical stripes.

Another way to change the look of an existing lampshade is to add "stripes" of trim to the shade vertically, along with the trim that you're using on the top and bottom rims. Not every shade will benefit from this type of trimming. In general, smaller shades will look great with stripes,

Five stripes of a flat braid trim add a definite zip to these sedate black lampshades; a small loop of the trim at the top rim and a fish tail cut at the bottom make these stripes very special.

as will shades that have definite "ribs"; but large shades may look a bit overdone with this treatment.

ESTIMATING & GLUING INSTRUCTIONS
for Vertical Stripes on Lampshades

1. Decide on the number of stripes you want to place on the shade. The size and style of your shade, and the lamp it's going on, will determine how many stripes will look best. As a guideline, four or five stripes usually work well.

2. Measure from the top to the bottom of the shade. Then, multiply that number by the number of stripes you plan to have to determine how much yardage you need for the trim. Include yardage to go around the top and bottom rims as well. The trim used for the stripes can be used on the rims, if it is not too wide ($\frac{1}{2}$", 1cm or less). Or it could be very interesting to use different trims for the rims and stripes.

3. When purchasing a trimming, always buy more than you need. Allow for a little creativity when working with stripes. You may want to add a loop at

the top, or let the trim extend beyond the edge of the shade. Experiment with the trimming before cutting it into the appropriate number of stripes.

4. For the spacing of the sections between the stripes, determine the circumference of the shade top by multiplying the diameter of the rim by 3.14 (pi, definition on page 51, item #3). Then, divide that figure by the number of stripes you plan to use. Do the same for the bottom rim. Assuming that the two rims are different sizes (as they almost always are), you will come out with two different figures.

5. If your shade has a seam, use that as your starting point. If there is no seam, establish a point where you will start on the top rim and directly below it, locate a starting point on the bottom rim.

6. On the top rim, divide the shade into four or five equal sections and mark those spots with straight pins, chalk, or pencil. Along the bottom rim, do the same thing: divide the shade rim into the same number of equal sections.

7. Check the guide marks to make sure that your stripes will be straight up and down. The marks at the top should be directly over the corresponding marks on the bottom rim.

8. Dot a line of glue, using a standard white glue, from one of the marks on the top rim to the corresponding mark on the bottom rim. Center a

stripe over the mark on the top and glue it to the shade.

9. Once all of the stripes have been glued in place, you can add your trim to the top and bottom rims, placing the trims over the ends of the vertical stripes.

A single vertical stripe.

As a variation on the stripe theme, especially for larger shades (and some smaller ones, too), use one row of a wide trim, around 2" to 3" (5 to 8cm) wide, centered on the front of the shade. This row can be made up of 2 to 4 layers of flat ribbon or fabric in varying widths used together, one on top of the other. Or, try a wide ribbon, alone or in combination, and edge it on both sides with a narrow type of contrast trim, such as soutache, rickrack, or fine cord. The narrow trim can be repeated on the top and bottom rims, and will look very handsome, indeed.

Diagram 7. To create a center stripe: Center a ribbon for the top layer over a wider ribbon. Add a row of gimp to each outside edge of the wide ribbon; then, add a row of soutache trim to each outside edge of the gimp. Glue a narrower gimp trim on the top and bottom rims.

∾ TYPE 3 ∾

Topper skirt.
Overlay an existing shade.

This technique gives a shade a really festive touch and makes a special statement in a room. What you will be doing in this instance is actually adding a separate "skirt" over an existing lampshade. This is a fast, easy item to sew and is quite a lot of fun to do.

Any small shade, but especially those of chandelier-size, is perfect for this decorative touch. Medium, as well as large-size shades, benefit equally from this styling (see the example of a large shade with a skirt on page 58). Again, it's important that you sit with your lamp — look at it, judge it, and decide if it and the room setting are suitable for a skirted shade. Keep in mind, this style can get a little cute or frolicsome, so it's important to pay attention to the details of the room environment. In the following areas a frolicsome touch can add a great deal to a chandelier or wall sconce:

❧ *Dining Rooms*
❧ *Breakfast Rooms*
❧ *Powder Rooms*
❧ *Entrance Halls or Galleries*
❧ *Bedrooms*
❧ *Children's Rooms*
❧ *Living Rooms*

The best type of shade for this treatment is a fabric or paper shade, that is translucent, as opposed to an opaque shade which allows light to come out only at the top and bottom of the shade.

Fabric Choices: Use a very light, sheer fabric, like organdy, batiste, or a synthetic sheer; or something with an open weave, such as net or lace.

GENERAL INSTRUCTIONS
for Making a Topper Skirt

1. First, you need to determine the length the skirt is going to be, by measuring the outside of the shade from the top to the bottom. Add an additional 1"(3cm) of fabric for hemming the top and bottom edges.

2. Next determine how much fabric you are going to need, by measuring the diameter of the top; multiply that number by 3.14 (pi definition on page 51, item #3) to find the circumference.

3. Take the circumference and multiply it by 1.5 or 2, depending on the fullness you want in the finished skirt.

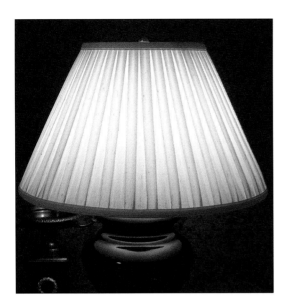

Above left: A standard box pleated fabric shade on a black ceramic lamp. *Above right:* The same lamp and shade, now with a topper skirt in a sheer fabric placed over the shade; flat braid trim finishes the top and bottom edges.

4. To gauge the amount of fullness you will want, evaluate how much "body" your fabric has. A lot of body means you should cut down on the fullness; while a softer, limp fabric will need more fabric to give it a nice, full look. Your guide should be two times the circumference for a nice fullness. You can always adjust the fullness later if you are unsure initially as to how the skirt will look.

5. Cut your fabric to the size you have measured (the skirt length by the width).

6. Take the piece of fabric and gather it along one long edge, this will be the top of the skirt. The gathers can be made either by machine or by hand. Pull up the stitching threads until the

top of the skirt is the correct size to fit over the top rim of the shade.

7. To finish the top edge, sew a piece of gimp or ribbon over the stitching. Hand tack, use a velcro dot or glue the skirt together at the top and add a separate bow, streamer, or special button at the join.

8. The easiest way to finish the bottom edge of the fabric is to use pinking shears and pink the edge.

9. Another way is to sew or glue a narrow trim onto the edge, such as rick-rack, soutache, a very narrow ribbon, or use the same trim that is on the top edge.

10. Another way to finish the bottom edge of the fabric is to trace a fine line of white

glue (slightly thinned) along the edge and sprinkle it with gold or silver glitter.

11. For even more glitter, dot the glue, in spaced intervals, over the surface of the skirt, then sprinkle little touches of glitter on the glue. You can substitute sequins, rhinestones, or anything else that glitters. But use a light hand with this treatment. Because, less is more.

SELECTING
LAMPSHADES

In the last few years lampshades have become available in a wider range of sizes and styles than ever before. I attribute this directly to the increased knowledge of consumers. Whatever the reason, your chances of finding an appropriately sized shade for your lamp are excellent.

Previously, you had to have a lampshade custom made or settle for whatever was on the lamp when it was purchased.

Having a lampshade custom made is still the best way to ensure the right proportions and the best quality. Ordering a custom-made lampshade gives you control over the size, the shade construction and style, the fabric, and, of course, the trimming. Although this is certainly more costly, when you think about the life of the lamp, which could easily be 20 to 30 years or longer (and with care the shade should last that long, too), then your investment certainly pays for itself over the years.

How do you determine the right size shade for your lamp?

1. If your table lamp or floor lamp has a shade on it and if it appears to be in good proportion to the lamp itself, take the shade with you to the store and ask for the closest size available to replace it.

2. If you cannot bring the shade with you, then measure it and take these measurements with you:

   a. measure the *diameter* of the *top rim.*

   b. measure the *diameter* of the *bottom rim.*

   c. measure the side of the shade from top to bottom, this is called the *slant.*

   d. place the shade on a flat surface and measure from the top of the rim straight down to the surface it's sitting on, this is called the *height.*

3. If the shade on the lamp is clearly not the right size or if there is no shade at all, take your lamp to the shop where you plan to purchase the new shade, so that you can get qualified guidance for a properly sized shade.

4. **As a general rule**, when you are at eye level with the shade positioned on the lamp, the bottom of the shade should

cover the metal stem that comes out of the top of the lamp. If it covers the lamp body too much, then the shade gives a top-heavy appearance to the lamp. If the shade is too short and you see a lot of the metal stem, the whole lamp has an unattractive look about it.

Study the photographs of lamps in this chapter to get a sense of how far down the shades should come onto the lamp base.

5. Let's say that you have a shade, and you know what you want changed about it, a larger bottom or a longer slant, etc. Take the measurements of the shade you have and make a rough sketch as I have done in Diagram 8. Use this to work with in the shop. It is always easier to show someone a sketch when selecting a new lamp shade.

6. If you decide to put shades on a chandelier or wall sconce where none exist, measure your *light fixture* and bring these measurements with you:

   a. *diameter* of the chandelier or *width* of the sconce,

   b. *height* of the fixture (do not include the chain of a chandelier in this measurement, and remember that you are always measuring the *widest* or *longest part* in any direction),

   c. if the fixture has "candles", measure the height of one from the top of the "candle" to the rim or cup that it sits in.

Special Note: Did you know that you can change the size of the "candle" by making it longer or shorter? You will need the help of an electrician, but it is a simple enough operation. Frequently, when a "candle" is taller than 5"(13cm), especially on chandeliers, it gets a leggy look that is out of proportion with the light fixture. A better height for a "candle" is between $3\frac{1}{2}$"(9cm) and 5"(13cm*)*.

Diagram 8. The different dimensions of a lampshade that determine the sizing of a shade.

The Size of the Harp

Most floor and table lamps contain a very important element that is called a *harp*. The harp is the curved metal piece that fits around the lightbulb and upon which the shade sits. In most lamps there is a *finial* screwed onto the top of it that serves to hold the lampshade securely in place.

Most people are unaware of the harp's importance, yet it is an essential ingredient in correct lampshade sizing. Look at the size of the harp on the lamp in the photograph on page 48. At 10" it is much too large for the scale of the lamp base. I switched to a 6½" harp (smallest size available for the correct proportions and scale of the shade that I selected for this lamp).

If you suspect that the harp on your lamp is too big or too small, pick out an assortment of harps (three or four in ½" [1cm] increments) to try on your lamp. The shopkeeper will usually let you return or exchange them until you have selected the right size. (Besides, they're inexpensive.) Keep trying different sizes until the shade looks right.

A store that sells lampshades will usually sell harps. Another source of harps could be a lamp parts supply shop or, sometimes, even a hardware store.

Recently, a (male) client, who I had supplied with quite a few lampshades, came to me and said, "I really couldn't understand why you were so insistent about getting the lampshades. Secretly, I was very much against it, but I gave in because I could see that it was important to you. And, NOW, I can't believe the difference they make in the room! How can people live without shades?" I should qualify that quote by adding that he had several chandeliers that were shade-less, as well some table lamps with sadly deteriorated lampshades. Not anymore!

Once the lamps in a room have properly proportioned lampshades, covered in appropriate fabrics with nice trimmings on them, it is easy to see what a beautiful, quiet impact they have on the ambience of a room.

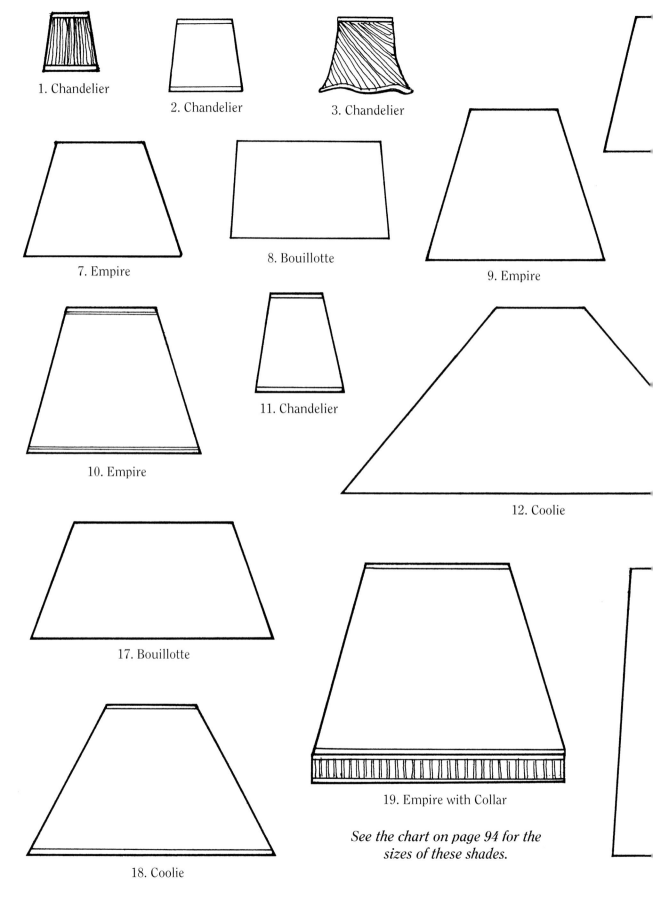

1. Chandelier

2. Chandelier

3. Chandelier

7. Empire

8. Bouillotte

9. Empire

10. Empire

11. Chandelier

12. Coolie

17. Bouillotte

18. Coolie

19. Empire with Collar

*See the chart on page 94 for the
sizes of these shades.*

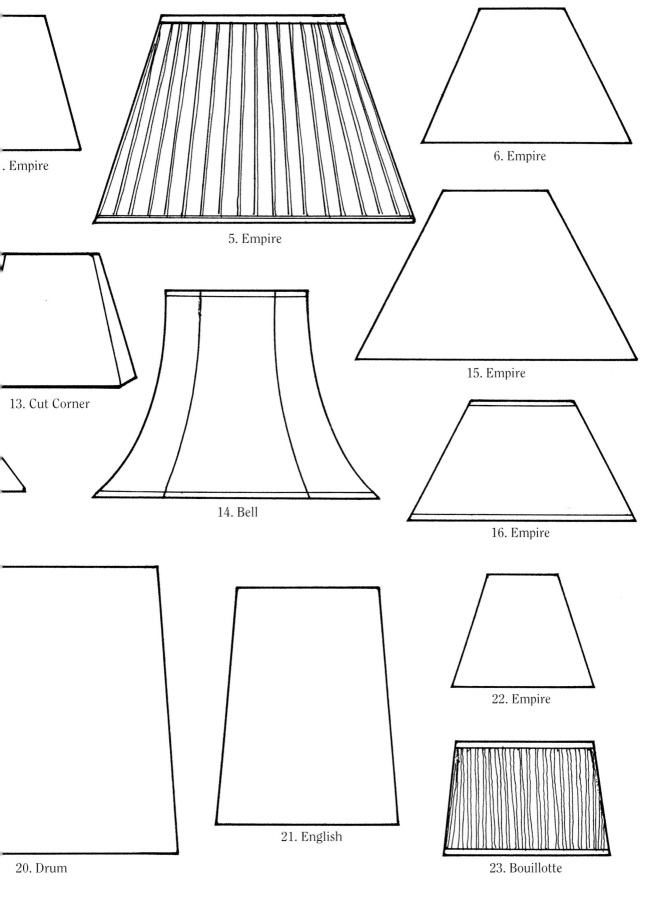

. Empire

5. Empire

6. Empire

13. Cut Corner

14. Bell

15. Empire

16. Empire

22. Empire

20. Drum

21. English

23. Bouillotte

BASKETS, TRAYS, AND BOXES

*D*id you know that baskets and trays can be your best decorating friends? Why, you ask? Because they are always there when you need them. Baskets and boxes, particularly, and trays, as well, are beautiful in and of themselves. As containers, they provide a decorative answer for, what I refer to as, the flotsam and jetsam of life.

*M*ail, newspapers and magazines, pencils and ballpoint pens, scraps of paper — it's these bits and pieces of "stuff" that seem to be the most difficult for us to control. After being in many homes, I venture to say that it is a lack of organization that creates the dilemma for most people. It's not fair, we say. **What are we supposed to do with it all?**

—Tip—

Organization is control.

Control is organization.

---

*I*n order to take charge of your "things," you must make an investment. First, you must invest some time and energy in dealing with accumulation. Then, applying the suggestions offered in this chapter, you will reestablish order in your household. What a triumphant feeling that is! I'll suggest several ways in which that can be done. There is no reason why organizing things in your home cannot be accomplished in an attractive manner.

A series of baskets used for tee shirts and sweaters, as well as handkerchiefs and belts in a closet area.

Magazines kept attractively under control in a medium-sized basket.

The following are suggestions for using baskets and trays for storing things in practical as well as decorative ways. Separate items by size, type, color, or subject.

TACTICAL PROCEDURE

1. Look around you. I know this may be painful, but we've got to go through it.

2. Try to see the loose items around you in terms of a common trait. Now, think of these items in terms of the four cate-gories below, and try to assign each item to a category. For instance, papers that are the same *size* (it doesn't matter what is on them), can all go into a basket.

Size: Newspapers, sweaters, tee shirts, dish towels, wash cloths, letter-sized paper, letters, school reports, business cards

3. Look at your things from the standpoint of *type.* In other words, groups of things that have to do with a particular activity. All of these can go into a basket. Collectively, they will determine the size and number of baskets needed.

Type: Hair products, items for bathing, toys (each child), anything broken, catalogues & brochures, writing equipment (pens, pencils, crayons & quills), shoe polishing items, glues, craft projects, ribbons and tags, stray & spare keys

4. You can also classify groups of things simply by *color* — this approach works best for textiles and wardrobe items. But you can also use this method for storing other items, like tennis balls.

Color: Hair bows, tee shirts, towels, scarves, belts, jewelry, wool skeins, fabrics, sweaters, gloves

5. If the above categories don't work for you, then look at everything from the standpoint of *subject.* Assign each item a subject. An example could be "accessories." Separate items in this way, and don't stop until every item has been given a label. Then plan a basket for each subject.

Subject: Bracelets, hairpins, mail, buttons, soaps, last year's Christmas cards, lingerie, sewing thread, bread and rolls, small potted plants, sets of keys, eyeglasses, paperclips, sport shoes

6. Use the suggestions below to help you start sorting. Depersonalize what the item may represent to you and look at it only from the standpoint of which category will best suit its purposes.

7. Once you have established a group or two, start collecting your baskets and enjoy the results!

—Tip—

Organization demands categorization.

❦ BASKETS ❧

Shallow, rectangular baskets

I find that rectangular, shallow baskets are a great way to organize loose items. At the same time, when you use several identical baskets together, you start to establish a "look" in your space.

1. Determine an appropriate size for your container — this is your *target size.* Take this size with you when you're shopping.

2. Determine the target size by measuring the things you want to store: the width, length, and height.

3. Allow at least an extra inch **in each measurement** for ease in fitting them into the basket.

4. Think of where you're going to place the baskets containing these items.

    a. If they're going to be set on open shelves or on the top of a table, desk or counter top, the quality of the basket material should be top-notch. Remember, you are creating a look here and it should be representative of your surroundings. For example, most of the woven fiber baskets,

❋ straw

❋ willow

❋ rush

❋ wood slat

❋ bamboo

look well in almost any space, except the most formal type of decor. Save the rougher, more unfinished textures for the closet or areas that aren't so "public."

b. Although baskets generally have a casual air about them, they also convey a timeless calm that makes them fit easily into many different surroundings. Sometimes clear lacquer is used as a finish coat and serves to deepen the natural color of the fibers. Sometimes baskets are painted. Lacquer or paint gives a more finished look to the basket. When finished this way, a basket develops a more sophisticated quality and can effectively be used almost anywhere.

c. When you consider where you are planning to put your baskets, think about how to get a contrast of materials between the basket and the surface it's going on. This will give a professional quality and provide even more visual satisfaction.

Contrast Studies

❋ *A rough woven rush basket sitting on a sleek stone or plastic laminate top*

❋ *A tightly woven wood slat basket on finished wood or glass surface*

❋ *A painted straw basket lined with a pretty linen towel placed on natural clay tiles*

❋ *A dark stained reed basket on old brick*

❋ *A soft texture on top of shiny lacquered cabinets*

Special Note: Sometimes you will come across baskets in nested sets, **when you do, grab them. They are invaluable when used stacked, one on top of the other, in closets or on shelves.**

Baskets with lids

Baskets with lids are ideal for the top of a desk, in a kitchen or bathroom, anywhere you want to put things away, have organization and a definite decorative look. Usually round in shape, they can also be found in oval, square, and rectangular shapes. They are excellent storage containers for such items as:

❋ *Hair ornaments, flowers, cotton balls, miscellaneous safety pins, straight pins, broken pins, and marbles;*

What a pretty and convenient carrier for holding eyeglasses and cases together.

❋ *odd knobs, pieces from a puzzle,
rubber bands, key rings, and spare
fasteners;*

❋ *ALL scraps of paper and match books;*

❋ *erasers, pencil stubs, clothes pins,
and pieces of string.*

Baskets with handles

Baskets with handles are my favorites. It's
probably because you can just pick them
up and take them anywhere. Whether the
handles are on the sides of the basket or
form a loop over the top; whether the bas-

kets are large or small, shallow or deep,
they just seem to have more of a decorative air about them.

I love the effect you get from tying a tassel
or chair tie around the handle of a basket.
Maybe it reminds me of the candy shop in
Chicago, where I spent my childhood. The
shop interiors were all white and I entered
a state of bliss every time I walked in the
door. Imagine being enveloped by the
smell of chocolate... The chocolate candies
layered between white sheets of paper were

kept in large, woven wood baskets. The baskets were painted in a fresh snowy-white shiny paint. Each basket had a handle and at the center of each handle was a big airy bow. The fabric was sheer and seemed to sparkle, in colors of pastel pinks and lavenders. A delicious memory!

A perfect setting for a large basket with handles is on the hearth of a fireplace. Although this is an ideal basket and setting for storing logs, this type of basket can also be filled with foliage. I find that the timeless look of a basket with a handle filled with flowers always adds charm to a room setting. Think of these items to use in a basket:

* *wild flowers*
* *grasses*
* *dried flowers*
* *flowers in pots*
* *boughs of fir trees*
* *branches from shrubs, bushes, or trees*

Bliss: a cat asleep in its own basket with its own bedcover (trimmed with a tassel fringe, of course).

- ❁ *branches with leaves or without leaves*
- ❁ *foliage with berries*
- ❁ *towels for the Bathroom*
- ❁ *towels for the Kitchen*
- ❁ *assorted hand soaps*
- ❁ *birthday or Christmas cards*
- ❁ *recent magazines*
- ❁ *assorted breadsticks and muffins.*

Special Note: Baskets of woven fibers do wear out if not cared for in a gentle manner. Don't overload them and attempt to carry them around filled.

Baskets are as individual as you are. When you find a beauty, use it with care, and plan to keep it for a long time.

Old-fashioned plain and twisted wire baskets serve the same purposes as already described. Today, sleek versions of wire basketry are readily available. The coated-wire types are available in colors and can make quite a statement when used in groups.

Consider grouping baskets together in rows along a counter top, or on shelves in a wall unit, bookshelf, or in a closet. You can also group them on the floor out of the way or under a table so that they're still visible to passers-by.

❧ TRAYS ❧

The uses of baskets and trays overlap a great deal. Trays can be substituted in many of the examples. There are certain areas, however, for which trays are preferable. Chief among them is when you want to display a collection of items or when you have a group of elements that you want to keep together in one spot.

In general, trays are available in a wide range of sizes, including very large varieties that are really meant to be displayed decoratively. Since the primary purpose of trays is to carry things, they are made of hardier materials: wood, metal, glass, plastic, papier-mâché, woven reeds, and stone; and in finishes of lacquer, paint, faux-any-thing-patterns and laminated fabrics.

Trays serve many practical uses and are also beautiful objects in and of themselves. When combined with other beautiful objects, the effect can be breathtaking. Imagine an antique silver tea service on a special tray. Or a unique collection of old and new perfume bottles on an antique silver tray.

Visually, a tray acts as an island, a special island. Treat it that way. You'll find that items on a tray can look special, even when they are not. Think of using a tray to:

* *neatly arrange your newspapers*
* *organize a group of desk accessories together*
* *show off a pair of candlesticks and a bowl*
* *keep wrapping papers and ribbon together and be able to move them out of the way for easy clean-up*
* *place a collection of peppermills*
* *stack current magazines into two or three piles*
* *display a collection of small glass animals or boxes*
* *keep your bedside table items in one attractive spot*
* *have a tray empty and waiting on a table in a Guest Room exclusively for personal belongings*
* *consolidate a needlework, sewing, or hobby project*
* *hold the pocket change that collects at the end of the day*

Think of using a tray as a portable desk. Keep a group of things on it that you tend

A collection of pepper mills on an old silver tray; a great way to keep pepper specks off the counters and table tops.

A beautiful antique oval tray holds a personal collection of old and new perfume bottles.

to move around. With the items all on one surface you can simply pick the tray up and move. You don't have to worry about where to stash things and scramble to gather them up at the last minute. When you want to change location, you simply pick up the tray and move. You also have the advantage of having everything placed on an attractive object, something others can admire.

Keep an eye out for old trays in your travels. Even if you find one in poor condition, don't discount it. A tray in a suitable material, such as wood or metal, can be restored. Don't pass up new trays, in new 20th Century colors and finishes, either. They can add an unexpected punch to an otherwise ordinary setting.

Small trays are great for tucking into unexpected places, like your dining table, close to the centerpiece, when it's set for company. People always need a place to put those things that inevitably surface even in the best of circumstances: a pit or seed, gum, a small bone, a bit of wax from the candles, a wedge of lemon or lime, and other things not worth mentioning.

Since trays don't wear out by themselves, and since one always seems to need a tray in a size not on hand, our acquisition of trays continues. The number of trays in the household keeps expanding, until one day you realize that you almost have a collection. That's when you should give serious thought to refining your buying habits and start acquiring trays based on quality as well as serviceability. After all, trays do make a delightful difference in the daily appearance of your household, and **their** appearance is important.

To keep accessories for the dining table handy, and to have light at times when you are not dining, try arranging these items together on a large tray. Attractive and, at the same time, easy to move when company comes.

✿ BOXES ✿

I don't think I've met a person yet who simply isn't crazy about boxes. Collecting boxes seems to be part of life. Someday I'm going to find out what it is about boxes that we find so irresistible and why we have this need to bring boxes into our lives.

Perhaps our love of boxes begins with the ease in which they can be placed in our surroundings. It seems wherever they're put, they improve the setting. I think of old boxes with a worn finish on a kitchen counter; polished wood boxes with books on a book shelf; pristine, highly refined boxes on a coffee table; a collection of petite porcelain boxes together on a silver tray; a wood and ivory antique box on a dresser.

No other subject seems to bring out the collecting instinct in us more than boxes.

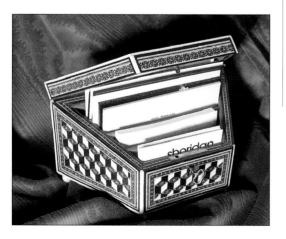

It just seems natural to keep acquiring them. With surprising frequency, they find their way into auction houses. If you're someone who really enjoys collecting boxes, I suggest keeping tabs on the auctions being held in your area. Also, take the time to frequent local tag and garage sales for unexpected finds.

Another reason for the popularity of boxes is the way in which different styles and periods of boxes blend together so naturally, whether used in a group or when placed throughout a room. Different sizes and finishes actually seem to complement each other.

I have found no limit in the styles and materials used for making boxes. And I've seen boxes so tiny they could be hidden in your hand or large enough to be called trunks. Many of the varieties of materials and finishes in which boxes are made are listed in the chart on page 78.

As we continue to accumulate with no end in sight, we need all the boxes we can

A trapezoidal inlaid Indian box from the turn of the century, which is perfectly suited to holding a current assortment of cards: greeting, personal enclosure, and business.

Various woods, shell, ivory, and china are materials all found in this charming group of antique boxes displayed on a granite top table.

get! We always seem to need another place to put things. Whether it's for your daily clean-up or for the moment when something (or someone) arrives unexpectedly and you must stow things quickly out of sight, boxes are the perfect answer.

Types: *Trinket, Jewelry, Tea-caddy, Bread, Toys, Tools, Trunk, Recipes, Make-up, Snuff, Biscuit, Coal, Sewing.*

Boxes are made in a vast range of sizes that can accommodate almost any thing that needs to be stored. In my opinion, one of their greatest attributes is that they can stand on their own and be lovely. They need not be filled with anything. Think of them as double agents...looking beautiful by themselves and all the while, inside, holding who-knows-what.

Shapes: *Round, Square, Rectangular, Octagonal, Hexagonal, Oval, Angled Sides, Tall, Short, Squat, Slim, Shaped-Top with: Pretty little feet, moulding, a lock and key.*

Materials:	Finishes:
Wood, all varieties: ordinary woods such as pine and oak to exotic zebrawood, satinwood, and burls	Rough, unfinished, worn, raw or smooth, waxed, polished, and clear lacquer finishes. Can be used as inlays.
Metal, all varieties: gold, silver, vermeil, pewter, tin, stainless steel, iron, brass	Polished, painted, unfinished, etched. Can be used as inlays.
Stone, varieties include marble, onyx, granite, agate, rock crystal	Polished, honed, unfinished. Can be used as inlays.
Glass, all types including mirror	Clear or colored, etched, cut
Lucite	Clear or colored
China and porcelain	Natural white, colored, painted
Animal	Bone, horn, shell, tusk; polished, natural finish
Applied cover	Fabric, paper, leather, suede
Interior Linings	Finished wood, suede, velvet or other fabrics; cork, metal, ivory or stone

Storage Ideas

Buttons; necklaces; broken eyeglasses and parts of same; broken pieces of anything (then you will always know where they are, even if you don't know what they belong to); pieces of string, rubber bands and broken shoelaces; keys: on rings, spares and unidentified; erasers, paperclips, matches, pencil ends, and stamps; thread, needles, pins, scissors, tailor's chalk, snaps, hooks and eyes, a small ruler; assorted sizes of colored post-its; pasta, macaroni or rice; a collection of marbles; potpourri; recipes; wrapped candies; tea bags; pens and pencils (working or non-working); stationery and papers of all categories; business cards.

I have found that a box is the most effective decorating tool for creating an instantaneous, lived-in, casual elegance. They have an air of always having been wherever-it-is they are placed. It's no accident that they have become the most-favored of all accessories for the home. ॐ

Left: Larger boxes look very good on the floor, whether empty or filled; the smaller box on the table does double duty by holding four place settings of flatware, making it easy to set the table for special get-togethers.

Below left: An antique two-drawer box, most likely made by a cabinetmaker for holding display samples of wood finishes to show to potential customers.
Below right: The same box, recycled for use today, is now the keeper of the jewels.

SCREENS

———————◆———————

*I*always pay homage to screens as the great, unsung heroes of interior decoration. No other item more profoundly affects the mood of a room, given its size and the small amount of space it requires. Adding a screen to a room instantly provides a professional finish to the whole decor. You might not realize that screens have been around for centuries, maybe even for thousands of years.

The ease with which they can be constructed must have been discovered early on and their quiet appeal reminds us that human beings have always had a need for privacy. I don't know of a better creative tool for creating privacy and separation in a space, while introducing a decorative element at the same time.

Look around your room....isn't there a corner that would look much better with a screen as an accent? Perhaps, there's an area in a room that could use a bit more separation, or an unappealing view that could be successfully disguised with the addition of a screen. Maybe you're simply in the mood for a change, but are not quite sure what to do.

When the desire for change strikes, think of bringing in a screen. It will provide your room with a strong new element that is also portable and alterable. If you have an existing screen somewhere on the premises, that perhaps has seen better days, I strongly suggest that you reexamine it for an overhaul. Renovating a screen, you will find, can usually be done easily and effectively.

The quiet elegance of an upholstered screen; one of a pair that flanks the floor-to-ceiling curtains in a Living Room.

—*Tip*—

If your general decor is in need of attention, add a screen to give it instant style.

A screen can serve many different purposes. I'm about to suggest some of those that might not have occurred to you. In the following suggestions a three or four-panel standing screen is the frame of reference. The *height* of screens, as well as the *width of the panels* can vary tremendously, but normally you can expect to find panels between 12" to 24" wide, and heights ranging from 60" to 84". Bear in mind that there are always exceptions to these "average sizes." If you plan to make a screen, of course, you can customize it to specifically fit your needs.

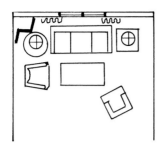

1. Place a screen diagonally in a corner of a room to instantly create an appealing, timeless look.

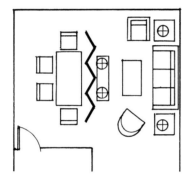

2. Stand one in the center of a room to divide the space into two areas. For this to be successful, the screen should be finished on both sides.

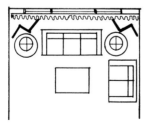

3. Take a pair of matching screens and use them to flank each side of a window instead of using draperies. For optimum effect, make sure the screens line up with the top of your window or the win-

dow treatment, or are close to the height of your ceiling.

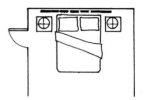

4. Instead of using a headboard, mount a screen to the wall behind the bed. In this case, the screen should be fully opened (flattened position). Ideally, the total width of the screen panels should be close to the measurement of the width of the bed. If it's off by a lot, consider using one less panel to bring the two widths closer together. You can also consider using a very wide screen (or two smaller screens together) and extend it the full distance behind both night tables and the bed.

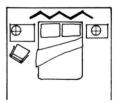

5. You can also stand the screen on the floor in its normal zig-zag configuration and use it as a headboard. In this instance, push the panels closer together or move them farther apart to get the screen to line up with the width of

the bed. The full extended width of the screen needs to exceed the measurement of the width of the bed enough to enable you to use the screen with the panels in the zig-zag formation. For additional instruction on this aspect, see Point **e.** under **Sizing A Screen.**

Using a screen as a headboard in this manner means you won't be able to lean against it. In my experience, many people don't use a headboard in a functional way; for example, lounging, reading, eating, watching TV, etc. Decide whether you want a decorative or functional headboard before planning to use a screen in this way.

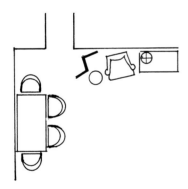

6. To direct traffic away from an unsightly view or a private area, set a screen in a line diagonally across the path of this area. You will successfully block off the part of the area that you don't want seen, without closing off the flow of traffic into the area.

7. You can use a screen behind a sofa in one of two ways:

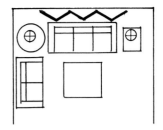

a. for a full height screen, stand it behind the sofa on the floor, with the panels either in a flattened straight line, or if the screen width is wide enough, stand the screen with the panels in a zig-zag position;

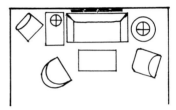

b. for a short screen, one that will fit in the space between the top of the sofa and the ceiling, mount it on the wall above the sofa, with the panels flattened, in a straight line.

Special Note: The technique of using a screen behind a sofa (as described in #7), can be especially helpful if your room lacks a strong "focal point." A strong "focal point" can be a fireplace, an unusual window or view, or some healthy architectural moulding. Every room needs a focal point to anchor the center of activity or attention. The focal point usually becomes the conversation area. The screen, then, acts as the focal point and indeed, can be quite dramatic, if it has some special quality.

A special quality could be any one or all of the following:

❀ *antique*

❀ *luxurious finish*

❀ *unusual color*

❀ *texture*

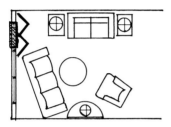

8. An unsightly air conditioner in a window can be successfully camouflaged by standing a screen in front of it. The screen should be slightly taller, by about 4"(10cm), than the top of the air conditioner. So that when you're in the room, you won't see the machine until you're right in front of it. As the cold air vent is located in the upper section of the air conditioner, the screen does not disturb the air flow. I find that using smaller panels, 12"(31cm) wide, for the screen does well in this situation, where the finished height will probably be around 48"(122cm). If you have a heating unit that is obtrusive and unattractive, try this idea to visually eliminate that piece of equipment. If your space permits, keep the screen on

an angle to the unit...it just looks better in the room that way.

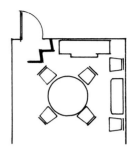

9. While we're on the subject of visually obscuring a distraction, if your central room has an open doorway through which you can see directly into a kitchen or bathroom, you may want a way to cut down on, if not completely block, the unattractive view. Stand a screen adjacent to the doorway opening, placing it on an angle, to hide a direct view into the room without disturbing the access into the room. You'll get the best results if the screen is as tall as, if not taller than, the top of the door frame leading into the unwanted area. This manner of using a screen usually requires that the screen be finished on both sides.

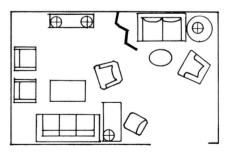

10. To create a special space within a room for greater privacy (for example, a spot

A short screen, covered with a faux bamboo wallpaper, conveniently disguises the air conditioner in a window behind it.

—Tip—

Always leave a few inches (7cm) between the screen and the piece of furniture so that it can "breathe."

A closer view, looking over the screen, of the air conditioner. The screen in no way affects the operating efficiency of the air conditioner.

An example of an exposed frame screen, with brass rings and fabric panels of beige silk, designed in the late sixties. Here it is used to visually separate the Dining Room from the Front Parlor. For a view of this screen decorated with striped panels, see the photograph on the cover of this book.

in which to sit with a friend or read), use a shorter screen, say around 60" (150cm). Place it on an angle to the area that you want to "create", close to a piece of furniture. Add a plant and enjoy.

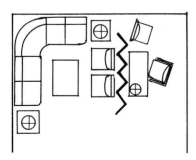

11. Again, a screen on the short side, 48" to 60"(122 to 150cm), can be positioned in front of a desk, or placed to the side, to create a separation from the rest of the space and give the person at the desk a degree of privacy without the formality of real separation. If the screen is going to be in front of the desk, take care to have the width of the screen standing in a zig-zag format the same as or wider than the width of the desk.

—*Tip*—

To increase the sense of privacy, increase the height of the screen.

Above left: An upholstered screen that, because it is seen from two sides, has been upholstered using different fabrics and different trims.

Above right: On the reverse side, the fabric gives a feeling of an old embossed leather, with antique nail heads for the trim.

Right: In this photo you can see the nail heads that were used on the "old" fabric side; the herringbone pattern, flat braid trim for the outer edges of the screen panels; and the welting that matches the pattern of squares in the fabric on the other side.

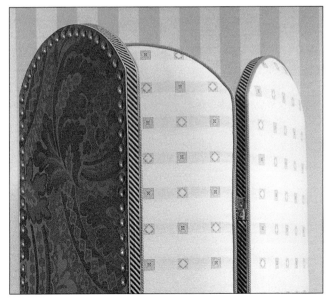

Special Note: To really show off a bit and be creative, put a stylish looking pedestal, at least 39"(99cm) high, in front of your screen — place it slightly off-center. Sit a wonderful sculpted bust or other piece of sculpture on the pedestal. A grand spectacular vase or special piece of pottery could complete the picture with equal panache. If the vase is not particularly special, fill it with large branches or an enormous bunch of flowers. They will look great.

Style Choices: When it comes to the selection of screens, choose a screen as you would a work of art for your walls. Here is how to focus your thinking in order to make a decision:

1. Look at the decor of the room where the screen is going. Imagine the screen standing where you think you would like it to be. Now ask yourself if you want the screen:

   ❋ *to be in contrast to the surroundings stylistically,*

   ❋ *to provide a dramatic counterpoint to what is taking place in the room,*

   ❋ *to be antique and look as if it's been there all along,*

   ❋ *or to have it quietly enter the space and just say "elegance?"*

2. Now consider style choices:

   ❋ *traditional, period antique or reproduction, Oriental, contemporary, architectural, Victorian, Art Deco, Art Nouveau, rustic*

   and materials:

   ❋ *wicker, straw, wood, bamboo, mirror, metal, glass, lacquer, fabric, painted canvas, contrast panels (different material from the frame of the screen).*

❦ SIZING A SCREEN ❧

It's also important to have a target size for the screen:

a. Use your ceiling height as the limit for the height of the screen and work down from that point.

b. Use approximate measurements...for example, if the screen is going to be used at a doorway and the doorway opening is 80"(203cm) high, then a screen measuring 82"(208cm) high or higher will be fine.

c. Do same thing for the width of the screen. Determine how much of an area you want the screen to cover by laying a measuring tape, a piece of string, or even a long scarf on the floor where you imagine the screen to be standing. This measurement becomes your target width of the screen.

d. The **number of panels** and the **width of each panel** are variables in the overall width of the screen. For example...the space that you want the screen to cover

Type of screen	Alteration
1. Fully upholstered	1. Recover with fabric, leather, or faux (vinyl) leather; use nailheads, ribbon, or a trim to finish edges of screen.
2. Exposed frame, contrast center of fabric, or other material	2. Paint or refinish the frame. Recover the center sections with fabric, faux (vinyl) leather, wallpaper, or paint in a contrast color.
3. Solid surface (including wood panels)	3. Paint, wallpaper, or cover with fabric. Or create a paneled effect by adding wood moulding or trim in rectangular panels. Edges of screen must be finished for a professional look: use nail heads, ribbon, or trim.
4. Exposed frame, see-through grill, or open-work center	4. Paint or refinish the frame. Add shirred or straight fabric panels behind the centers by attaching rods, top and bottom, to each screen panel.
5. One-sided fabric or canvas covered frame	5. Recover or upholster over existing material; or convert to a double-sided screen by covering or upholstering the reverse side; use fabric, faux(vinyl) leather, or even paint.

is about two/thirds or three/quarters of the actual width of the screen itself when it is fully extended.

e. To illustrate: If the distance you want to cover is about 36"(92cm), then a screen whose overall width measures around 48"(122cm) will be perfect. This could be a 4-panel screen, each panel being 12"(30cm) wide; or it could also be a 3-panel screen with panels that measure

16" to 18"(41 to 46cm) wide. However, a 3-panel screen with 12"(30cm) panels would not work in this example.

Altering a Screen

Most screens lend themselves to being altered very easily. All you need is the courage to try an idea, patience, and clean

Another find. This time from the Salvation Army. What seemed to be an uninspiring four-panel wood screen with open cut-out motifs, was transformed with a few coats of soft, blushy pink enamel paint, and now looks fabulous standing next to a desk.

hands. If your screen is very tall and/or heavy, the best way to work on it is with the screen in its upright, standing position (as opposed to lying it down) with a footstool for you to stand on. Other, smaller screens that are easier to handle, can be worked on either in a prone position on a table or the floor, or in an upright position.

Special Note: You can make a totally personal statement by hand painting a fabric or canvas yourself (or by making arrangements to have this done for you), and using the finished fabric to cover/recover a screen. If this concept appeals to you and you want to create the panels yourself, but you don't have a screen, then have one made: an open wood frame construction with hinged panels, in a size and height to suit your particular requirements.

The concept behind "Instant Decor" is that everyone can make certain changes to his or her interior space that will improve its appearance and uplift his or her spirits. Little things can change a space to a far greater degree than either the size or the cost of the item would indicate. Of course, some things can be done on one's own, but projects of a larger nature will sometimes require the assistance of a professional designer or decorator.

When larger issues arise, there are many advantages to working with a professional designer. Because of the designer's ability to see things from a design standpoint and because most things that need to be done are of a problem solving nature, the designer/decorator can quickly cut through a lot of the unimportant issues that tend to impede the decision-making process of the non-professional. The result in most cases is usually a reduction in the cost of the project.

It is to your advantage to develop and maintain a relationship with a professional designer, the same as you would with a doctor. For in the end, no one will know as much about you and your way of life than your designer/decorator (not even your hairdresser), because design is all about living.

Everyone needs and deserves an interior environment that complements and enhances his or her lifestyle. It's a perfectly healthy instinct to want to be surrounded by nice things. To my way of thinking, decorating is as much a part of daily life as eating.

The subject of decoration is such a happy one for me, that I can't imagine that everyone isn't dreaming up things to do all the time!

Lots of people do, of course. But I realize that not everyone knows what or how to dream. So I have tried to develop ways to expand your senses so that dreaming is not only made easy, but becomes an inseparable element in your daily life. This translates into comfort and joy in your surroundings, for years to come and beyond. Make the most of it.

Metric Conversion chart

cm.	in.	cm.	in.	in.	cm.	in.	cm.
1	$^3/_8$	16	$6\ ^1/_4$	$^1/_{16}$	0.16	1	2.54
2	$^3/_4$	17	$6\ ^3/_4$	$^1/_8$	0.32	2	5.08
3	$1\ ^1/_8$	18	$7\ ^1/_8$	$^3/_{16}$	0.48	3	7.62
4	$1\ ^5/_8$	19	$7\ ^1/_2$	$^1/_4$	0.64	4	10.16
5	2	20	$7\ ^7/_8$	$^5/_{16}$	0.79	5	12.70
6	$2\ ^3/_8$	21	$8\ ^1/_4$	$^3/_8$	0.95	6	15.24
7	$2\ ^3/_4$	22	$8\ ^5/_8$	$^7/_{16}$	1.11	7	17.78
8	$3\ ^1/_8$	23	9	$^1/_2$	1.27	8	20.32
9	$3\ ^1/_2$	24	$9\ ^1/_2$	$^9/_{16}$	1.43	9	22.86
10	$3\ ^7/_8$	25	$9\ ^7/_8$	$^5/_8$	1.59	10	25.40
11	$4\ ^3/_8$	26	$10\ ^1/_4$	$^{11}/_{16}$	1.75	11	27.94
12	$4\ ^3/_4$	27	$10\ ^5/_8$	$^3/_4$	1.91	12	30.48
13	$5\ ^1/_8$	28	11	$^{13}/_{16}$	2.06		
14	$5\ ^1/_2$	29	$11\ ^3/_8$	$^7/_8$	2.22		
15	$5\ ^7/_8$	30	$11\ ^3/_4$	$^{15}/_{16}$	2.38		

When you know	*Multiply by*	*To find*
inches	2.54	centimeters
centimeters	0.3937	inches

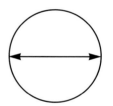

Diameter of a circle
Circumference = diameter x π
(π = 3.14159265359)

Table of Lampshade Sizes (Keyed to drawings on pages 62–63)

DIAMETER TOP RIM	DIAMETER BOTTOM RIM	SLANT		DIAMETER TOP RIM	DIAMETER BOTTOM RIM	SLANT
1. 2" (5cm)	3"(8cm)	3"(8cm)	13.	5"(13cm)	8"(20cm)	7.5"(19cm)
2. 3"(8cm)	4"(10cm)	4"(10cm)	14.	8"(20cm)	16"(41cm)	5.5"(14cm)
3. 3"(8cm)	5"(13cm)	4.25"(10cm)	15.	6"(16cm)	16"(41cm)	10"(25cm)
4. 7"(18cm)	11"(28cm)	7.5"(19cm)	16.	6"(16cm)	13"(33cm)	7.5"(19cm)
5. 10"(25cm)	18"(46cm)	12"(30cm)	17.	9"(23cm)	13.5"(34cm)	6.5"(17cm)
6. 4"(10cm)	12"(30cm)	8"(21cm)	18.	5"(13cm)	14"(36cm)	9"(23cm)
7. 5"(13cm)	9"(23cm)	6.5"(16cm)	19.	8"(21cm)	14"(36cm)	11"(28cm)
8. 8"(23cm)	9"(23cm)	12"(30cm)	20.	14"(36cm)	16"(41cm)	16"(41cm)
9. 5"(13cm)	10"(25cm)	9"(23cm)	21.	8"(21cm)	10"(25cm)	13"(33cm)
10. 5"(13cm)	10"(25cm)	8.5"(22cm)	22.	4"(10cm)	8"(21cm)	6.5"(16cm)
11. 3"(8cm)	5"(13cm)	5.5"(13cm)	23.	8"(20cm)	9.5"(24cm)	6"(15cm)
12. 5"(13cm)	22"(56cm)	13"(33cm)				

❧ CREDITS ☙

(Listed in alphabetical order.)

Agostino Antiques, Ltd.
Antique furniture, reproductions, and accessories. Pgs. 77, 88

Beatrice Designs, Inc.
Decorative home accessories. Pgs. 71, 81

Bill Rothschild, photographer. Pgs. 29, 81

Boussac of France, Inc.
Fabrics. Pgs. 13, 55, 79

C.M. Offray & Son, Inc.
Woven trimmings. Pg. 89

Century Furniture Industries
Upholstered furniture, tables, accessories. Front cover, pgs. 3, 7, 41, 43

Christofle Silver, Inc.
Flatware. Pg. 88

Decorators Walk
Furniture, decorative accessories. Front cover, pgs. 7, 29, 67, 81, 58

Dominic Castellanos
Painting and papering. Pgs. 10, 14, 24, 83

France Voiles Company, Inc.
Sheer fabrics. Pg. 83

F. Schumacher & Co.
Fabrics, trimmings, wallpapers, and wallpaper borders. Pgs. 3, 7, 9, 10, 14, 15, 19, 21, 32, 33, 36-37, 41, 43, 45, 55, 58, 76, 83

Interiors by Robert
Drapery and upholstery fabrications. Front cover, pgs. 7, 9, 19, 55, 83, 88

John Boone, Inc.
Accessories, tables. Pg. 83

J. Pocker & Son
Framed pictures and prints. Front cover

Julia Gray Ltd.
Antique and reproduction furniture, and accessories. Pg. 88

Oriental Lampshade Co., Inc.
Lampshades. Pgs. 49, 88

Royal Doulton USA Inc.
Tableware. Pg. 88

Saxony Carpet Company, Inc.
Area rugs. Front cover, pgs. 3, 9, 19

Scalamandré
Fabrics, trimmings, and wallpaper borders. Pgs. 13, 14, 17, 19, 23, 31, 33, 34, 35, 36–37, 38, 47, 52, 53, 88

Standard Trimming Company
Trimmings. Pgs. 17, 29, 33, 49

Steve Miller, Woodworking
Electrical work. Pg. 88

Victor Carl Antiques
Chandelier. Pg. 88

Waverly
Fabrics and wallpaper borders. Pgs. 10, 15, 24, 41, 43, 49

Yale R. Burge Antiques, Inc.
Antique furniture and accessories, reproductions. Pgs. 3, 33, 74, 76, 77, 88

ᏞᎧ Acknowledgements ᏉᏉ

It would be impossible to imagine writing this series of books on decorating without the cooperation, kindness, and genuine desire to help that so many, many people in the Interior Design Industry have extended to me. I wish there were room to thank each and every one of you individually, but for now I shall confine myself as follows:

For always being available and graciously offering whatever I seemed to need at the moment, I am truly indebted to:

> *The staff in the New York showroom of F. Schumacher & Co.; the staff in the New York showroom and at the mill of Scalamandré; the staff at Yale R. Burge Antiques; the staff at the New York showroom of Century Furniture; and the staff in the New York showroom of Boussac of France.*

For providing advice, back-up support, and professional guidance, I would like to specially thank:

> *Giselle Barreau-Freeman; Adriana Bitter; Linda Blair, ASID; Robert Boccard; Rinat Lavi; Kirk Phillips; Joan Rice; John Sarando; Patricia Sullivan; and Bebe Winkler, ASID.*

But most of all, I would like to acknowledge the love and single-minded conviction of my parents, Dr. Stuart Grayson, and my dear friend, Ellen L. Vanook. ᛦ